LAP

DISCARD

Habitats around the World

Rain Forest Life

by Janine Scott

CAPSTONE PRESS
a capstone imprint

Pebble Plus is published by Capstone Press,
151 Good Counsel Drive, P.O. Box 669, Mankato, Minnesota 56002.
www.capstonepub.com

Books published by Capstone Press are manufactured with paper
containing at least 10 percent post-consumer waste.

Library of Congress Cataloging-in-Publication Data
Scott, Janine.
  Rain forest life / by Janine Scott.
     p. cm. — (Pebble plus. Habitats around the world)
  Includes bibliographical references and index.
  Summary: "Color photos and simple text describe animals and their adaptations to a rain forest habitat"—Provided by
publisher.
  ISBN 978-1-4296-6815-6 (library binding)
  ISBN 978-1-4296-7152-1 (paperback)
  1. Rain forest animals—Adaptation—Juvenile literature. 2. Rain forest ecology—Juvenile literature. I. Title.
II. Series.
  QL112.S397 2012
  591.734—dc22   2011005317

Editorial Credits
Gillia Olson, editor; Lori Bye, designer; Svetlana Zhurkin, media researcher; Laura Manthe, production specialist

Photo Credits
Dreamstime/Steven Francis, cover
Minden Pictures/NPL/Alex Hyde, 13
Picture Window Books, 6–7
Shutterstock/Alan Kraft, 5; Dr. Morley Read, 14–15, 17, 21 (top); ecoventurestravel, 10–11; Edwin Verin, 18–19; Kerry
     Banazek, 20; Luis Louro, 1; worldswildlifewonders, 9
Visuals Unlimited/Thomas Marent, 21 (bottom)

Note to Parents and Teachers

The Habitats around the World series supports national science standards related to life science.
This book describes and illustrates animals that live in the rain forest. The images support early
readers in understanding the text. The repetition of words and phrases helps early readers learn
new words. This book also introduces early readers to subject-specific vocabulary words, which
are defined in the Glossary section. Early readers may need assistance to read some words and to
use the Table of Contents, Glossary, Read More, Internet Sites, and Index sections of the book.

Printed in the United States of America in North Mankato, Minnesota.
032011   006110CGF11

Table of Contents

Warm and Steamy

Tropical rain forests are hot, steamy places. It rains nearly every day. These areas of thick trees and plants are home to millions of animal species.

Layers

Rain forests have four layers. The emergent layer is very tall trees. The canopy is the rest of the treetops. The understory and forest floor are the bottom layers.

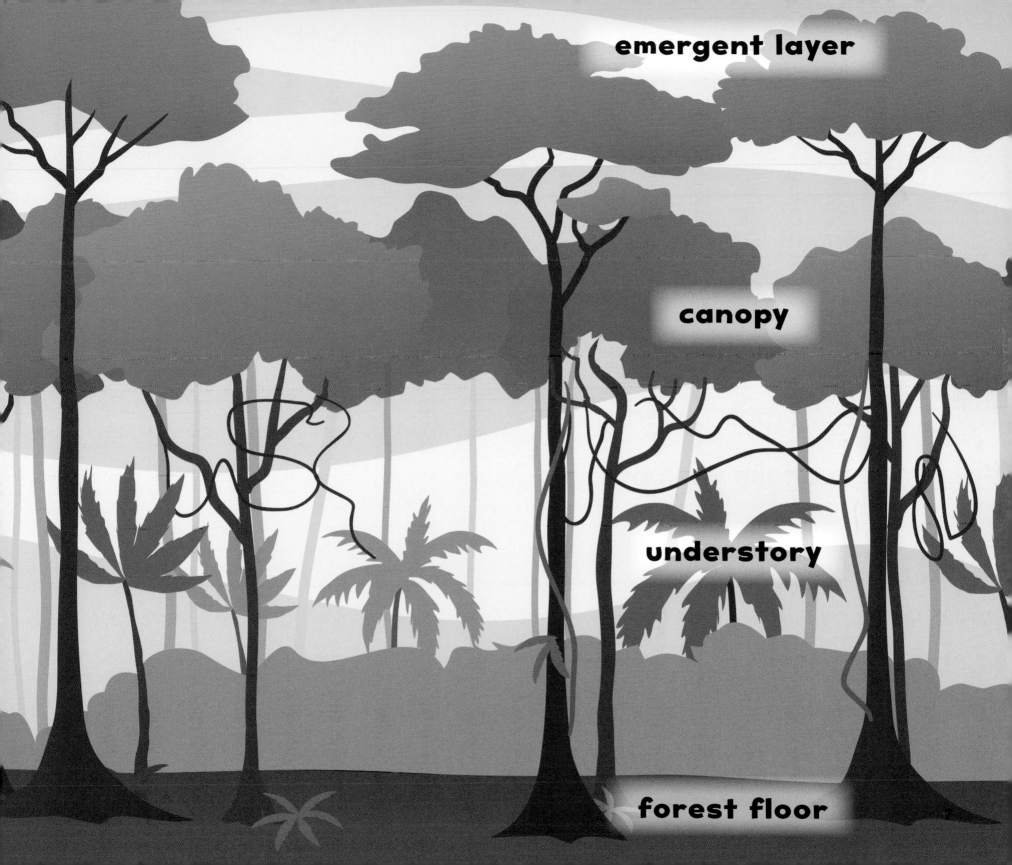

Emergent Layer

The rain forest's tallest trees push out of the canopy in the emergent layer. Harpy eagles and morpho butterflies fly through the treetops.

Canopy

There are lots of leaves and fruit to eat in the canopy. Spider and howler monkeys swing through the trees. Macaws and toucans nest here.

spider monkey

Understory

The darker understory is
a good place to hide.
Stick insects fool predators and
prey by looking like branches.
Vine snakes look like vines.

stick insect

In Between

Some animals move between layers. Jaguars wait on tree branches for prey to come by. Tree frogs have sticky toe pads to climb tree trunks.

Forest Floor

Animals on the forest floor
are good at living in the dark.
Ants and beetles tunnel through
the soil. Coral snakes use smell
to find prey.

Full of Life

Rain forests hold about half of the world's species of animals. More are found every day. Imagine what new animals we'll find in the future!

Fun Facts

- The largest tropical rain forest is the Amazon rain forest in South America. It covers more than 2.3 million square miles (6 million square kilometers).

- Temperate rain forests are cooler than tropical rain forests. Temperate rain forests can be found on North America's West Coast from northern California to British Columbia, Canada.

Leaf-cutter ants cut pieces out of leaves with their jaws. Every year, these ants cut down almost 20 percent of the leaves in a rain forest.

The harpy eagle weighs only 20 pounds (9 kilograms), but it has feet the size of an adult man!

A jaguar's spots help it blend in. The spots look like leaf shadows in the dim light of the forest.

Glossary

canopy—the layer of leaves and branches made by the tops of tall trees in a forest

emergent layer—the top layer of a rain forest made up of the tallest trees

predator—an animal that hunts and eats other animals

prey—an animal hunted by another animal for food

species—a group of animals with similar features; members of a species can mate and produce young

tropical—hot and wet

understory—the area below the canopy in a forest; small trees, shrubs, and plants grow in the understory

vine—a plant with a long stem that clings to the ground, a tree, or another item as it grows

Read More

Fredericks, Anthony D. *A Is for Anaconda: A Rainforest Alphabet.* Chelsea, Mich.: Sleeping Bear Press, 2009.

Mitchell, Susan K. *The Rainforest Grew All Around.* Mount Pleasant, S.C.: Sylvan Dell Pub., 2007.

Salas, Laura Purdie. *Rain Forests: Gardens of Green.* Amazing Science: Ecosystems. Minneapolis: Picture Window Books, 2007.

Internet Sites

FactHound offers a safe, fun way to find Internet sites related to this book. All of the sites on FactHound have been researched by our staff.

Here's all you do:

Visit *www.facthound.com*

Type in this code: 9781429668156

Super-cool stuff! Check out projects, games and lots more at www.capstonekids.com

Index

Word Count: 203 (main text)
Grade: 1
Early-Intervention Level: 18